Great Gorillas

Madison Parker

GROWING UP WILD

NorwoodHouse Press

Cataloging-in-Publication Data

Names: Parker, Madison.
Title: Great gorillas / Madison Parker.
Description: Buffalo, NY : Norwood House Press, 2026. | Series: Growing up wild | Includes glossary and index.
Identifiers: ISBN 9781978574052 (pbk.) | ISBN 9781978574069 (library bound) | ISBN 9781978574076 (ebook)
Subjects: LCSH: Gorilla--Juvenile literature. | Gorilla--Infancy--Juvenile literature.
Classification: LCC SF408.6.A64 P375 2026 | DDC 599.884--dc23

Published in 2026 by
Norwood House Press
2544 Clinton Street
Buffalo, NY 14224

Designer: Rhea Magaro
Editor: Kim Thompson

Photo credits: Cover, pp. 1, 5 GUDKOV ANDREY/Shutterstock.com; p. 6 Igoroorine/Dreamstime.com; pp. 8, 9 LMspencer/Shutterstock.com; p. 10 Ryan M. Bolton/Shutterstock.com; p. 11 Eei_tony/Dreamstime.com; p. 13 Eric Gevaert/Shutterstock.com; p. 14 Trek Bears Photography/Shutterstock.com; p. 15 Apgestoso/Dreamstime.com; p. 17 Kiki Dohmeier/Shutterstock.com; p. 18 DejaVuDesigns/Shutterstock.com;p. 19 Papa Bravo/Shutterstock.com;. 21 Hung Chung Chih/Shutterstock.com;

Printed in the United States of America

TABLE OF CONTENTS

Great Gorillas

Gorillas grow up in the **wild**.

Baby gorillas are called infants.

How Baby Gorillas Look

Infants are born with little hair.

They have **pale** gray skin.

Baby gorillas have a powerful **grip**.

They also have a strong **sense** of smell.

How Baby Gorillas Sound

Baby gorillas live in family groups. They **communicate** with other gorillas.

They **grunt** and hoot when they are happy. They cry when they need help.

What Baby Gorillas Eat

Infants drink their mothers’ milk for two or three years.

Gorillas are **herbivores**.

Babies learn to eat plants.

They eat leaves and twigs.

They eat fruit and **bamboo**.

Lots to Learn

When they are about three months old, baby gorillas start to explore. They pick things up. They play.

Baby gorillas learn by **imitating** others.

When they are about eight months old, they begin to climb trees.

All Grown Up

When they are about eight years old, young gorillas are **mature**.

Adult males lead family groups. They are called silverbacks.

Glossary

bamboo (bam-BOO): a tropical plant with a hollow, woody stem

communicate (kuh-MYOO-ni-kate): to share information and feelings

grip (grip): the ability to hold on to things

grunt (gruhnt): to make a short, low sound

herbivores (HUR-buh-vorz): animals that eat only plants

imitating (IM-i-tay-ting): copying what others do

mature (muh-CHOOR): fully grown or developed; adult

pale (payl): light in color; not bright

sense (sense): the ability to learn about your surroundings by smelling, hearing, tasting, or seeing

wild (wilde): natural places where no people live

Thinking Questions

1. What are baby gorillas called?
2. At what age do baby gorillas start climbing?
3. What do adult gorillas eat?
4. How do gorillas communicate with their group?
5. What is the name for mature male gorilla leaders?

Index

About the Author

Madison Parker spent her childhood in the city of Chicago, Illinois. A farm girl at heart, today she lives in Wisconsin with her husband and four children on a small farm with cows, goats, chickens, and two miniature horses named Harley and David. Her favorite dessert is vanilla frozen custard with rainbow sprinkles, even in the winter.